PONDERABLES

Poems on Worms, Souls, Baseball,
and Other Important Topics

RP Ericksen

PONDERABLES

Poems on Worms, Souls, Baseball, and Other Important Topics

iUniverse books may be ordered through booksellers or by contacting:

iUniverse
1663 Liberty Drive
Bloomington, IN 47403
www.iuniverse.com
1-800-Authors (1-800-288-4677)

ISBN: 978-1-4917-6685-9 (sc)
ISBN: 978-1-4917-6686-6 (e)

Library of Congress Control Number: 2015907256

Print information available on the last page.

iUniverse rev. date: 05/13/2014

In the belief that we face mostly ponderables, not imponderables, this book of poems ponders a few ideas, some aspects of poetry and, finally, the end itself. Any elements some readers might find obscure—Wittgenstein, for example, the omphalos, or the Apostle Paul's poem on love—can be googled, as you readers already know. Any elements some readers might find slightly offensive will, I hope, be appreciated by others. As I suggest in my poem on Whitman, I believe a poet chooses a topic and then tries to be honest.

Contents

TAKING IT UNDER 1

MAKING IT SEEM ENOUGH 2

WHERE'S WITTGENSTEIN? 3

MALINOWSKI 4

NOAH'S ARK 5

MY MOTHER TONGUE 6

THE BRINY DEEP 7

GRIEVE NOT TOO LONG 8

NEVER TILT ALONE 9

THE BLESSINGS OF A GYROSCOPE 10

THE CANDY CONSENSUS 11

IT'S ONLY SEX 13

WALLACE, IDAHO 15

THE LION OF AMSTERDAM 16

FOCUS 18

THE HARDENED EDGE 19

OUR ESSENCE 20

MINIMALISM 21

THE MARINERS IN 2004 22

MOTHER 24

THE WORM AND I 26

WINTER'S GROWTH 27

THE BINGE 28

MY BODY 29

A FRIEND OF MIDDLE YEARS 30

TULIPS 32

R.G. SWINBURNE AND THE SOUL 33

TRANSPLANTATION, TRANSMIGRATION 34

MY WALLET AND THE POPE 36

INTERROGATING HEAVEN 38

BIRDSONG 39

FAITH 40

WHEN RELIGION RAN RED 42

CONSULTANT ON METAPHOR 44

WOULD-BE SOMNIAC 45

SIEGFRIED 46

IN PRAISE OF PREJUDICE? 48

IN SEARCH OF THE COMBUSTIBLE 49

CARBONATED 50

HARE AND HOUND ALIKE 51

GAINING WEIGHT IN AFRICA 52

THE SECOND TIME 53

TINTERN TO BRECON 54

SINGING THE BLUES IN BERLIN 56

QUESTIONED AT SCHIPHOL 57

MONEY: FOUR DEGREES OF SEPARATION 59

DERIVATIVES 60

ATLAS SHRUGGED 61

NAMES AND ADDRESSES 62

ZAUBERBERG..64

EISBEIN MIT KRAUT 66

NARCISSUS ON HOLIDAY 67

SO IRONIC WE MIGHT RUST 68

BLUE JEANS AND THE ELECTRIC GUITAR 69

YPRES.. 71

LICKING OUR WOUNDS WITH A SEPTIC TONGUE..................72

THE KNUCKLEBALL 74

MELOS, MY LAI, ABU GHRAIB 75

COLOR COMMENTARY ON AMERICAN WARS......................77

SIMPLE TRUTHS..79

NOTE TO SELF: HYDRATE 81

REMEMBERING WALT 82

THE DICKINSON EFFECT..83

THE HEMINGWAY CODA.. 84

DID THEY DO IT TOO? 85

A RIFF ON PAUL 86

REAL POETRY 87

SMITTEN 88

PROPER POESY? 89

LES MURRAY, MORE MATTER.................................... 90

LOUIS AND THE *ARS POETICA*..*91*
GRAVITY..92
GOOD FRIDAYS..93
SLIPSTREAMING...94
RETRAIN OR RETIRE? 95
NINTH INNING IN PANKOW 96
THE GRATEFUL DEAD 97
DANSE MACABRE...98
OBIT IN THE TIMES 99
TABLE OF CONTENTS..100

TAKING IT UNDER

What do you undertake,
and why? What do I?
Too much? Too little?
With too blithe a spirit?
Too somber?

And where is the under
where you take it?
A rock, a bushel?
Down Under, under cover?
Under advisement, under a veil,
or out in the open?

Examine these things,
lest the life you live
be that unexamined one,
the one said not to be worth living,

lest that which you undertake
in your indeterminate number
of coiled days falls short,
or falls long, the blitheness quotient
over or undershot

on that day when your undertakings
meet your undertaker,
he who takes you under
to a place of his choosing,
for good, or at least forever.

MAKING IT SEEM ENOUGH

The amplitude of finitude
is measured out in minutes,
one or two the limit
sans air, sans pump,

yet I, as eager as any
for a large harvest,
think roughly of years,
not keeping track of months,
much less my weeks or my hours,

careless often
of minutes like this,
careless of so many of their fellows,
though the pleasure in each
can be ample,

careless of beauty,
careless of meaning,
careless of connections
which mean the earth to me,

until this morning,
repentant as a sinner in a tent,
bright sunshine and
clear summer air at dawn
shaking me by my lapels,
making my minutes
momentarily expand,

large thoughts
clambering over small.

WHERE'S WITTGENSTEIN?

I got a little tight last night,
which is to say loose,
the contents of my skull
rattling at random,
like pebbles in a hubcap,

contents not in the sense
of protoplasm, that gray matter
resembling a discolored head of cauliflower,
but rather the electrical impulses
seeking to focus on an idea,
or a piece of information,
grabbing that idea and pulling it across a synapse,
like a clerk in a warehouse store,
locating an item on the top shelf
in aisle eighteen,

though all my efforts by late last night
were rather half-hearted,
which has nothing to do, of course,
with some half of that muscle
which pumps blood out of my chest cavity,
but has more to do with my emotions,
my intensity of feeling and commitment,
the physical locus of which I cannot begin to locate,
though it surely has little to do
with the pump embedded in my ribcage,
despite my forebears' wholehearted use of "heart"
in this manner for millennia.

So much of what we say is blather.
Maybe it doesn't matter.
Or does it help explain those teachers
of a six-thousand-year-old earth?
Or those who'd give Sarah Palin a berth
in the ship of state?

MALINOWSKI

Malinowski spoke to me this morning,
whispered from the dusty shelves.
Born in Krakow when my grandmother
was but a toddler in Norway,
he who later taught at my alma mater,

Malinowski sang to me
in the measured melodies of modernity,
brought me back to my modernist self,
explained in modulated tones
the Melanesian mythologies,

the matriarchal dream of a stalactite
opening a path to the First Mother's womb,
letting the spirit of a baby
enter and grow,

the Melanesian belief
that spirits still enter
the womb of the mother,
producing life.

I recognize, once again,
the colorful nature of pre-modern beliefs,
explanations devoid of scientific insight,
and I know, courtesy this time of Malinowski,

that science and reason are better,
more likely, really, to get it right,
in contrast to strange myths
from the dim past,
the six-day creation,
the spirit probing Mary's womb.

NOAH'S ARK

For all those hoping to find Noah's Ark
somewhere in the Middle East,
some rudiments of a boat
high up on land, to prove the Bible true,
I warn you that some will scoff,

will wonder if this is Noah's boat,
or just a boat, for many such
might have been made in ancient times,
and it seems unlikely that Noah
will have signed his name
on the keel or the gunnel,

nor will the pairs of animals have been
checked off by type and number,
two of each, with their cabin designated,
so that the proof you seek may not suffice,
but if you could

find an ancient man or woman,
either would do, sans omphalos,
I and others would be forced
to recognize Adam or Eve,
the first and only pair in no need
of an umbilical cord,

a creationist's dream evidence, and,
though skin usually disappears over time,
a loving God, who might like some day
to teach a lesson to all those
who write "Darwin" inside their fish,
and add four legs,

could well have taught mummification
after the Fall, or arranged just the right
level of dry heat to leave those smooth,
unperforated bellies intact.

MY MOTHER TONGUE

What is destined for English, my mother tongue
since my mother's mother left her Swedish shores?
Will it, like Latin, survive a thousand years or more,
uniting a continent, or the known world,
long after England and America have disappeared?

Corrupted by its use among the many,
through army camps and brothels,
through air traffic control towers,
through Coke, Camels, technical manuals,
lingua franca for entire continents
of those with other tongues, yet recognizable
to the sharply attuned ear,

will it later limp along as a dead language,
known to the eye if not the ear,
our Virgil, our Ovid, our *Caesar's Wars*
read by school children, even though
"I came, I saw, I conquered" might leave
"mission accomplished" ever so slightly
in the shade? Or do we really believe

our empire so benign, so beloved, so capable,
so in harmony with the wishes
of our tribal god, that we will never die,
our mother tongue the language of the court
on Judgment Day? In words once uttered

by a legislator opposed to bilingual education:
"If English was good enough for Jesus,
it is good enough for me."
Perhaps that speech will be recalled
by our Cicero, by our Tacitus,
and listed under "irony"
in some future grade school text.

THE BRINY DEEP

What old man of the sea
does not remember
the briny deep in which
he took his form,

sprouted fingers, sprouted toes,
thought, perhaps, that soon his nose
would seek out air and change him,
sea creature to land mammal,
landed, yet drawn to water,
drawn to men in boats?

Vestigial memories little understood,
that vague desire to drink a drink
in Copenhagen, be tattooed
in Singapore.

GRIEVE NOT TOO LONG

Grieve not too long at the grave.
Grieve not too long, or gravity
will pull at your thoughts,

gravity, that ephemeral force,
unseen, will pull at thoughts unseen,
and your loiter at the grave

will drag you down. Better
to let dead thoughts, dead plans,
and other dead alone,

thoughtlessly, to save the thoughts
which rise up to soften that grief
engraved upon your flesh,

lest gravity, the great equalizer,
tug and pull at your grief
and bring it to its fellows underground.

NEVER TILT ALONE

Who would not choose to have
one's own Sancho Panza,
the sort of fellow who,

despite an occasional thirst
and an eagerness to fill out
the last notches on his belt,
despite a practiced eye for grim reality
and a willingness to give advice,

remains ever sympathetic and loyal,
through the occasional foible,
the odd peccadillo, remains ready
to tolerate one's lifelong pursuit
of Dulcinee, remains ready, at the end,

to parry the jibes of the multitude,
to loosen one's armor, place a pillow
under one's head against the stony ground,
and name all madness merely
a great nobility of soul.

THE BLESSINGS OF A GYROSCOPE

Once upon a time I turned,
turned from knowing
how to strike a nail,
where to set a two-by-four,

set upon a new course,
tempest-tossed, tied to the mast,
compass a-swivel. Only
the spinning gyroscope stayed true,

and so I've bounced off continents,
suffered a bruise or two,
floated in pure bliss,
licked the frosting
when cake did not taste sweet enough.

Bulging girth, you ask?
Mostly mirth. Satisfied.

THE CANDY CONSENSUS

Most of us probably agree
on our assessment of candy:
attractive, though too much can be cloying,
or at least bad for our health.
Whether one's candy is laced with sugar
or laced with chocolate, whether it is
melt-in-the-mouth fudge, ice cream, or crème brulee,
we are not likely to think it a diet in itself,
or entirely approved by our dentist or doctor.

So where does eye candy
fit into this picture?
What is sweet, male or female?
Why does it change over time,
in body type or hair on the chest,
and can there be too much
of a good thing? Does too much
eye candy cloy or make you ill?

Is ear candy to be noted and feared
in the sweetly commercial side
of Paul McCartney, but never in Bob Dylan?
In Mozart but not in Schoenberg?
Can too much Mozart make you ill?

Nose candy is notorious, of course,
the thrill of a moment, costly, illegal,
with a little something to fear
in terms of addiction. Or is this
form of dessert mainly deplored
by the Puritan, who seems
a little down on candy of any sort?

Consensus tends to break down
as we broaden our gaze,
as we ponder the universe of pleasure.
Skin candy is to some

the most alarming of all.
Too much silk or cashmere
will never do.

IT'S ONLY SEX

What if I said that Mozart's Queen of the Night
curls my toes as no other queen?
What if I claimed that Mozart and some of his dead pals
burrow paths into my brain, tickle the pleasure receptacles,
give me orgasmic pleasure that no other combination
of tone, rhythm and harmony can easily match,
and what if I were to claim approximately the same
for Jagger's "Satisfaction," vibrating my body,
a struck match on the tinderbox of desire,
for Lennon's "Imagine," resonating in my soul,
the purest hymn of our generation,
for Dylan's "Lost in Juarez," scratching and stroking
my memories of youth?
Could I then allow you your Nine Inch Nails
or even your Andrew Lloyd Weber?

What if I told you a gin and tonic
can slide down very easily,
as can alternative ingestibles
and altered states of mind,
that I have savored both corned beef and hash?
Would you condemn alike the gin mills of old London
and the damage of crack cocaine,
or, when you just say no to drugs,
would you stamp your foot and shake another martini?

What if you thought of sex
as mainly a gift of pleasure,
and what if you got past all the taboos
and considered, with closed eyes,
stroke and response, stroke and response?
Could you then imagine, in a restricted market,
choosing that pleasure over no pleasure,
allowing that pleasure to those who choose?

Can each taboo be crossed as easily as admitting

a fondness for the Everly Brothers?
Is it more than a question of health and safety?
Does each avatar of taboo really deserve
a self-appointed place in God's righteous army?
It's only sex. It's only drugs. It's only rock and roll.

WALLACE, IDAHO

He was just fourteen,
this grocery boy from Wallace,
now a mid-years man
visiting the bordello-turned-museum
where he had once brought provisions,

adding his stories
to those of the guide,
the time he bent over,
setting down a box,
tight pants exposing
his plumber's bum,

when a warm finger
probed his perforation,
making him stand up straight,
employees of the house
rubbing up against him,
making him blush,

and he told us all
of their ambition,
one working her way
through veterinary school,
fine young women, friendly,
women with purpose
behind their southern strategy,
offering tours
of their southern hemisphere
for a price.

THE LION OF AMSTERDAM

[For Arthur Wicks, *in memoriam*]

He pissed round the edges
of a property in Seattle,
the place his sire and dam called home.

He prowled halfway round the world
in his day, which, when you think of it,
is about as far away as you can go,
in his case with paw prints
from New Orleans to Prague,
from Rio to Aberystwyth,

but I always wanted to beard this lion
in his spiritual den at Amsterdam,
where Jesuits hold high Latin mass
every Sunday at eleven,
where windows suffuse the streets
in a warm, pink glow, seven nights a week,
where genever can be backed by a beer
in old brown bars, day in day out,
where minds can be altered and moods enhanced
for a handful of coins and the striking of a match,

though this lion was recovering from a wound,
hobbled one day in New Orleans,
the first healing softened for eighty-four hours
by self-administered morphine,
and then the regimen of perco this and oxy that,
climbing down the ladder, until, to his surprise,
he'd lost his taste for meat, lost his thirst,

and some might have thought this old lion
ready to lie down, ready to rest his white mane on a pillow,
but when I tracked him to the banks of the Singel Canal,
when I followed his spoor
like a photographer for National Geographic,
I found his wily skills undiminished,
his slightly limping gait graceful yet,
his quiet, gentle saunter down old paths
still the object of admiration all round,
his somewhat muffled roar sounding forth
at more than a poem a day.

FOCUS

Focus is everything, they say,
how you spend your time,
where you send your thoughts:
family or friends,
vocation or avocation,
this world or the next.

Some say it is whether
you button your buttons
and wear matching socks,
whether you live in a dream world
or embed in the one that is real,

but I say that I would have missed
a chat with Churchill last night,
sharing a drink. The night before
I raised my father from the dead
and cared for him. Who would miss that,
or the time my doctor father
pinched my left cheek?

Though dreams can be frustrating at times,
walking knee-deep in sand,
and then the water rises and you
can't quite swim to the opposite shore,
this too shall pass away.

Edison and Einstein didn't get
to where they are today (or where they were
last week, having a drink with me
at my club), by buttoning every button
or matching every sock.

THE HARDENED EDGE

It's not easy at my age
to hone the hard edge
of discipline.

Responsibilities
accumulate over time,
with papers to be read,
grades to be recorded,
emails to be sent,
tasks to be attended
as chair of this or head of that,

not to mention piles of paper
stacked on the desk,
slipped into boxes, as needed,
spread round the room,
wheat with the chaff,

so that it takes
the character of a saint,
the discipline of an Augustine,
the will of a Simeon Stylites
to let these things simmer and bubble,
to locate yet another back burner,

saving the precious hours of the day
for reading, musing, sitting in a chair,
placing an occasional, carefully-chosen
set of words on paper, that which gives joy
to be guarded at all cost.

OUR ESSENCE

When we seek the unique
in homo erectus,
some would say the brain,
some the opposable thumb,
but I would submit the crease
that hides our pucker,

this six or eight inch vertical gash,
a mark of bipedalism
not to be found
in any four-legged creature,

more distinctive to the species
than the two protrusions in front,
flaccid but yet apparent
in the female monkey or ape,
or the pouch and garden hose
adorning the mammalian male.

Those two cheeks,
kissing each other,
unless we're picking a flower
or crouched for evacuation,
more indicative
of the non-anorexic human
than any other feature,
surely fundamental.
No ifs or ands, we are butts.

MINIMALISM

Whenever a pitcher "runs out of gas"
or has "nothing left in the tank,"
I wonder about all the wasted fuel.
I wonder about Juan Marichal of old,
kicking at the eye of God, or Mike Mussina,
nose bent to the ground, furtively looking
for something in the grass.
Most of their successors today
fidget in their own way,
all of them carefully winding up,

and all of this after Don Larsen,
he of the perfect game, and that
on the high altar of the World Series,
taught us his lesson in minimalism,

the calm and stoic look toward home,
the explosive push off the rubber,
the whip of the arm,
the planting of both feet,
and then the replication.

In more than half a century,
no one's learned from Don,
suggesting we're not wired for minimalism,
suggesting we could as easily expect
a college student to spend four years
focused on curricular activities
or the rest of us to place our energy
only where it most belongs.

Perhaps there's a natural, necessary
coefficient of wastage, so that
Juan Marichal's ballet and
Mike Mussina's mime are simply
the decoration, the plumage
that helps to make life good.

THE MARINERS IN 2004

Poor Edgar. In every one hundred times at the plate
he is getting twenty-five hits, seventy-five outs,
a rotten year, and even if he stings the ball
on those twenty-five happy occasions,
he's hitting two-fifty, and when he
actually stings the ball, a screaming line drive
to the right field corner, bases loaded, two outs,
a should-be double changing the game, plus
three more rbi on his maybe-Hall-of-Fame totals,
if the right fielder is especially fleet and limber,
picking the ball off his shoe tops at full gallop,
it is a nullity and not one of those five extra hits
in every one hundred at bats that would rescue Edgar
from failure and add another year
to his contract and career.

And poor Bob Melvin. This second-year skipper
inherited the plummiest of plum jobs
and looked like a winner for four months of his first six,
but is now plagued with an entire roster of players
lacking three hits in every one hundred at bats,
and even if every one of them can catch the ball
ninety-five times out of a hundred
when it touches his glove, that is still not ninety-eight,
and who knows how many times it should have
touched his glove, but he was a step slow,
or took a first step the wrong direction,
or how often the outfielder will throw it
three miles over the head of the cutoff man,
costing a run but not even a bad mark on his ledger,

so Bob Melvin soon will be fired
and we fans in the Pacific Northwest
are suffering minor depression, wondering if maybe
the game falls apart only at that point
when we turn on the television. Or maybe

it was bad luck to attend the second game of the season,
the one where they got battered and set the tone,
and all of this in a game where on defense
you can be successful ninety-five percent of the time
and be rotten, and on offense
you can fail seventy percent of the time and be great,
but if bad luck follows you five times in a hundred,
you never even break into the bigs.

This tells me that I'm designating myself a hitter,
and if I manage to accomplish something
three days out of every ten, or please
thirty students of every one hundred,
that is not failure, but a mark of pride,
and I'm a hall-of-famer in my own eyes,
perhaps to no one's surprise,
whether my team wins or loses.

MOTHER

When does Mother Nature
cry out in anger or despair?
Surely not this morning,
as she coaxes me along
a green-leafed, tree-trunk-gnarled trail,
roar of the Pacific lingering in the air.

This is no virgin forest.
Mother may have wept a bit
some years ago, when the roar of ripping saws
rang in her ears, but this Mother
cannot be accused of any fixation
on virginity, and the luxuriant salal leaves
beside a tracery of nursing logs
under shadowed green
seem pure enough today,

until I wet them with my waste
and wonder, briefly,
in some Kantian reflection,
whether I have sinned,
though surely other animals
have sinned the same,
and I, alone among my species
on this October day,
cannot really soil a forest,
can only enrich the soil
as Mother intended, she who's changed
many a soiled diaper in her day,
with no revulsion.

But does she, perhaps, share my revulsion
when I return from the forest,
drink my morning coffee, and read news
about Congress and the EPA?
Breathtaking in their focus on filthy lucre,

they preside over a soiling
that will not wash away
and most certainly does not
enrich the soil.

THE WORM AND I

Edible though we may be in the end,
food for worms, and edible
though worms may be to some,
protein, as they say, even tasty,
I find it, rather, incredible,
to think myself on either side
of that food chain.

Neither a borrower nor a lender be,
wrote the Bard, and I am loath
to lend or borrow at that banquet table,
not hungry enough to dine
so directly from the earth,
and not yet ready to feed the soil.

I watch the odd robin or sparrow
make of the worm a delicacy,
that worm in turn watching me
think myself outside the great chain of being,
as we humans are wont to do,
and possibly knowing better.

WINTER'S GROWTH

In this winter
of my discontent,
the larger pants I had purchased
to accommodate growth
grew snug,

for I have shored up donuts
against my ruin,
comfort foods have comforted me,
the nicer pastries at Starbucks
a wedge against ennui,

the only questions now
whether spring will follow
and whether summer
can bear the weight.

THE BINGE

Singed by a binge,
hectored and vectored
back to the straight
and the narrow
by that little cricket
on my shoulder,

I now kiss the straight,
pledge myself to the narrow,
reformed once more,
and entirely committed

to reform again,
as needed.

MY BODY

My body is a source of pleasure,
or has been, in my homo erectus
desire to reproduce, even when
reproduction has been thwarted
aforethought, my body tricked,
but pleased,

tricked also into planning for winter,
eating in preparation for the hunt,
though my hunt has taken place
largely indoors, the extra
fat and salt and sugar
unnecessary pleasure,

and I have remained unrepentant
for forty years or more,
though repentance now
has put me on my knees
a time or two, despite
faux hunts in the gym
and other tactics of evasion,

my body as source of pleasure
compromised, less certain,
a lifelong is destined to be was.

A FRIEND OF MIDDLE YEARS

I have found a friend
in middle years, a close friend,
a new friend, if we measure life
by decades. We've grown together
for ten years or more, so that now
we're never apart.

We've had good times, he and I,
marked by regular visits
to the vineyard and the malt yard.
We're always relaxed together,
convivial, sharing in all the good
that life has to offer,

in liquid form and otherwise,
enjoying often the many delightful
variations on salt, sugar, and fat
that never lose their ability to please.

We travel together, at home and abroad,
and find ourselves just now in London,
the scene of my youth, my student years.
I tell him how good it was
to be young and lean,

living life energetically, nimbly,
in Penny Lane and Strawberry Fields,
in the bright optimism of youth,
with a little less of the substance
of middle years weighing me down.

We are jogging now, up at first light,
still on Seattle time. I take him
in the freshness of a June morning
down Oxford Street, to Marble Arch,
south through Hyde Park, back
toward Piccadilly, and there, after passing
the Ritz and the Royal Academy of Art,

I glance sideways into shop windows,
see my friend running,
slightly in front, bouncing
just a little up and down,

and I vow secretly
to leave him behind,
leave him here in England,
run with him daily,
but starve him a bit
of that food and drink
which have so sustained our friendship.

I know I will miss him
on the flight home,
but the seat will seem less cramped.

TULIPS

Today the tulips
have gone all slack, and,
though it is only April,
though their splashes of color still delight,
I can see they are not long
for this world.

It seems barely a week
since they were young,
girls schooled in a convent,
tightly wrapped, guarding their treasure,

and now they are loose-limbed bawds,
careless, clothes disheveled.
I can smell their whiskey breath,
though it is not yet noon.

I must remember
their path has been mapped
by God or nature. So many
young virgins cannot have changed
through perversity alone.

Their tightly wrapped petals
opened when they were meant to,
responding by design,
delighting the eye,
basking in the warmth,
drinking in the sunlight,

and, though they now pass their prime,
it was not the drink that did it,
nor the openness to life,
but that part of life which cycles,
that part which recycles us all.

R.G. SWINBURNE AND THE SOUL

Dotty old Professor Swinburne, named to a chair,
mounted a podium at Oxford years ago
and floated bubbles of balderdash
into the air, a mile wide and half an inch deep.
The soul, he said, must certainly exist,
must certainly survive beyond the grave,
a reality subject to scientific proof, he said.
Just look at the urges, feelings, and memories
which make up my reality outside my physical being,
outside my corporeality. Surely this non-physical reality,
that which I am, will live on
after my physical reality rots away.

What rot, I say, the sort of rot which I,
a young student shaped by Teutonic rigor,
felt able to denounce from the back row.
"Poppycock," I said, using a word
which had wormed its way
into my consciousness, burrowing a little hole
into my synapses, into my gray matter,
one little niche of meaning among the many,
among the urges, feelings, and memories
which will rot away, along with their physical container,
sometime after my death,

so that, in the paradigm of Swinburne,
in his claim for certainty of the soul,
my immortal soul resides most completely,
most permanently, in my thumb drive,
a physical object which will not rot away
upon my death, but will retain, then as now,
my urges, feelings, memories,
every word I've written over many years,
and every word I will write
in the years to come.

Thumb drives of the world, rise up,
for yours is the kingdom of heaven.

TRANSPLANTATION, TRANSMIGRATION

[Swinburne #2]

Dotty old Professor Swinburne,
while searching for the human soul,
caved in to empirical science in matters of the heart,
recognizing that Christian Barnard and his scalpel
have put the lie to that old claim,
"My heart is true to you,"
when my heart lies in a bag of medical waste,
and it is Joe's heart now which yet remains true,

so that loving you or loving God,
with all my heart and all my soul,
the latter finds itself in need of a new locus,
and our professor
imagines a more complex surgery,
sometime in the future,
in which my brain might fill that bag of waste,
yet I can love you still, with Joe's brain as my apparatus.

Thus the clever professor
posits my identity, my soul, my non-physical essence
capable of migrating to another hard drive,
a modern transmigration, which he considers proof
that my soul is immaterial, and also, by God, eternal,

though I balk a bit,
wondering how easily Joe's brain
will replicate those paths
by which certain words, like "poppycock,"
and certain sounds from Puccini and the Beatles,
plus the works of Soren Kierkegaard
and memories of a particular moment, a particular face,
have wormed their way into mine,
worms burrowing paths into my brain
so completely, so uniquely,
I rather think that I am the worms,
these worms which constitute my soul,

so that when and if my body
should ever harbor Joe's brain,
I will have said goodbye,
while another batch of worms,
in that bag of medical waste or in the ground,
enters my brain and places my soul at rest.

MY WALLET AND THE POPE

My backside could not have been
more exposed, had I been
a baboon in stocks, had I painted it red
and placed both hands on the floor,

so that the artful dodger
who pushed from behind
as I entered the crowded metro
at Piazza del Popolo,
one heavy bag in each hand,
had very little need
for the skill and courage
attributed to the Roman cutpurse,

and I, momentarily off my guard,
aware only of the one or two things
I can now keep in focus at any one time,
and those one or two things
having aroused my travel-weary indignation,

I was divested, and can only hope
he was caring for a small and sickly child,
that he represented in some fashion
all the theatrical beggars
I had finally learned to pass by,
the palsied, the mounds of human misery
huddled under blankets,
holding out their shaking cup
and a kitschy picture of Jesus.

This might then explain
why Karol Wojtyla's blessing,
so generously offered as I looked up
from St. Peter's Square,
had so quickly lost its power to protect—
within hours no cash, no cards,

merciless cabbies,
in their exquisite torture
of circuitous back alleys,
stealing the last bills from my front pocket—

or maybe it was some deficiency
in my state of belief.

INTERROGATING HEAVEN

How does heaven function?
This simple question
waxes complex
the more we parse
the parameters of bliss.

The food? The drink?
Weather patterns?
Forms of entertainment?
Will the brilliant complexity
of human waste evacuation
fall into disuse?
Do the decrepit
return to youth?
Dead babies
have a chance to grow?
With which spouse
is one fated
to spend eternal life?
How does heaven function?

Some say that ever since
Vikings buried boats
and Egyptians buried beer,
heaven has functioned as
a human, all-too-human ploy,
mitigating loss, softening sadness,
facing down the finality
of fearful death,
and nothing more.

BIRDSONG

At dawn today
the shriek of cormorants
captured my attention,

for reasons I do not know.
Perhaps they were quarreling
over breakfast, or maybe

reading today's stories
about Republicans in Congress,
but when I cocked my ear

to listen, I could hear
not just the brass of cormorants,
but woodwinds and strings,

an orchestra of birdsong
completely undetected moments before,
which made me wonder

when we quit listening
for angels and elves,
or the voice of God herself,

and whether my sudden acuity
for birdsong might represent
an epiphany to those of us

who rarely cock our ear
toward God or unseen spirits,
with the difference, of course,

that if I turned your attention
to background birdsong,
you would hear it too.

FAITH

There is a faith cozy
within the confines of reason,
a faith which respects
pre-modern mythologies,

but only to mine them
for lingering values,
not in search of cosmology,
but of ancient wisdom and perennial truths.

Will such a faith sell, some ask,
as if that were a meaningful critique,
as if overflowing churches
bear testimony to truth or value,

churches which preach a risen Jesus
who wants to lower your taxes,
protect your right to keep and bear arms,
and make sure gays cannot marry.

Try selling a compassionate Jesus
to West Coast Americans in 1942,
those who knew the shape
of a truly American eye,

those who trained
their truly American eyes
on Japanese-American properties
soon to be sold cut-rate at auction,

or try selling property law
to traveling Europeans in 1492,
the Spanish who stole gold in Peru,
the Pilgrims who stole land at Plymouth Rock.

Selling isn't everything,
as even Jesus might have said,

if we were to mine his words
for lingering values and perennial truths.

Perhaps the Jesus who sells best
is not the best Jesus.

WHEN RELIGION RAN RED

Once upon a time,
religion ran red,
during that sanguinary
red dawn of history,

fifty thousand years or more
when primitive men
with primitive knives
sliced open primitive hearts
to appease their primitive gods,

so that Abraham and Isaac,
in a story which made
Kierkegaard's blood run cold,
represent in fact a happy transition,
the taking of human sacrifice off the altar,

and *Iphigenia in Tauris*,
as told by Christoph "Bald Willie" Gluck,
though the rust red dancers
and rust red chorus
cavorting under rust red walls
seem ready only to mute
the red blood about to spurt
from the imposing high altar,
ends with bodies intact,

as if Gluck, and Aeschylus before him,
noted that Agamemnon,
sacrificing Iphigenia to the gods,
he murdered in turn by Clytemnestra,
enraged at the loss of her daughter,
she done in by Orestes to avenge his father,
left only a large pool of blood
reddening the dawn of history,

a dawn we have since tried to leave behind,
our urge toward private retribution restrained by law,
our religious rituals more symbolic,
less sanguinary, except for the traces of red
still to be found in the primitive Osama,
and his primitive counterpart, George.

CONSULTANT ON METAPHOR

When I counseled young Yeshua on metaphor,
I tried to warn him against double meaning,
the tilt that can go negative,

"fishers of men," for example,
a brilliant image, but does one want to imply
that one sets the hook or entangles people in nets
against their will? Consider it
through the eyes of the fish, I said,
as you did so well with lilies of the field,

and then there is "bread of life,"
so intimate, so nurturing, so filled with promise,
but think for a moment of those millennia
in which religious belief tutored the cannibal.

I can't begin to describe how I worried, later,
when young Mahmoud insisted on "jihad."

WOULD-BE SOMNIAC

In my struggle, once again, for somnia,
three a.m., ears surging
to the rhythm of my pulse,
thoughts a-jumble, innards dealing
with my last repast,

I ponder the great ones,
Aristotle, Archimedes,
Ben Franklin, Babe Ruth,
and wonder if they too
had nights like this,

or whether the balm of genius—
the wisdom of the Golden Mean,
the power of the well-placed lever,
Poor Richard's Almanac,
the sixty home runs—

might have assuaged
and left them with the sleep of babes.

SIEGFRIED

First darkness, then silence
broken only by those patrons
who think this the best time to cough,
like sounding their horn in a tunnel,
or clear their throats, as if
they were the ones about to sing,
until finally the quiet is complete.

The curtain rises on a small, dark man
in leather apron, the only sound
his file rasping on steel,
intensity of sound, controlled sound,
a soon-to-be-growing wall of sound,
slowly adding each voice in the orchestra,
each voice on stage, intensity unbroken
for five short hours,

save for an interval glass of wine,
coffee, a sweet, and ruminations
on the sad fact that Wagner preceded Adolf
in that one dark, secret thought,
ignorance passing for wisdom,
envy passing for idealism,

the thought that there exists
a small, dark race which covets gold,
which covets power,
which seeks out secret power
to control the world,
and thus stands in *our* path
toward wealth, power,
and world domination.

But if we listen to the music
and savor the delights on stage,
the dragon, the flames, the talking bird,
if we vibrate with the wall of sound
and simply indulge the adolescence
of that silly boy,

we can understand
why even some Israelis
now listen to Wagner.

IN PRAISE OF PREJUDICE?

Some rise in praise of prejudice,
implicitly, not openly,
mostly unwitting students
of Herder and Gadamer,
who say it tutors us to like like,
it nurtures human bonds.

Many mainline
Herder and Gadamer,
though their texts be unknown,
liking like a natural condition,
the sweet siren song
of fascism, subtle,
submerged, seductive—

no certain taint,
Herder, after all,
spreading his wisdom
long before the Nazis,
Gadamer lingering long after—

the harder lessons of democracy
so easy to ignore. Not everyone
who says "Lord, Lord," will enter
the kingdom of heaven,
not every avatar of freedom
knows the meaning of the word,

yet human progress takes a step
with every narrow circle broken,
liking like crude and easy,
in every family, every cave,
liking and living with unlike
the only path toward those two little words
so often incanted, so often ignored,
"peace" is one, "justice" the other.

IN SEARCH OF THE COMBUSTIBLE

Homo Sapien, clever as a button,
barely learned to use fire
before he began looking
for more things to burn,
first twigs and branches,
then trees, whole forests,
occasionally a neighbor's
thatched roof,
a neighbor's children,
a rival prophet,
sometimes burning for comfort,
often for pleasure,

and over time his cleverness
only increased, shiny black rocks
from the bowels of the earth,
then oil, distilled within
an inch of its life, ignited by spark,
the whole internal combustion thing,

infernal to some,
those who value air to breathe,
those who urge us
to make friends with the sun
before the sun, its warmth captured
by our homemade greenhouse,
makes crisp bacon of us all.

CARBONATED

How to live
a carbonated life,
a life with bubbles,
a life with fizz,
yet use less carbon?

We Americans,
we who yearn to travel,
yearn to condition our air,
we who now shape
our carbon footprint
in ten-league boots?

And, God help us,
here come the Chinese,
the Shanghai skyline of Pudong
lit up like an electronic billboard,
skyscrapers doubling
as computer screens,
commercial messages
flashed into the night,
Manhattan, by contrast,
dull and quiet.

Plenty of bubbles,
plenty of fizz.
Enough excitement
to warm the world.

HARE AND HOUND ALIKE

Hare and hound alike
sprint to their destinations,
sprint at breakneck pace,
however capricious
those destinations might seem,
however subject
to instant change,

and I too emulate the hare,
model the hound,
though I grow gray
sprinting from place to place,
from Beijing to Alsace,
another summer gone
on the scent of something,

the scent of wine and *terroir*
in Colmar, scents beyond imagination
in Beijing, each destination
seeming important at the time.

Another summer gone,
and I, panting for breath,
dream of the tortoise,
admire the pug.

GAINING WEIGHT IN AFRICA

Gaining weight in Africa?
The weight of experience, perhaps,
and a load of guilt, certainly,
for any discerning visitor,

acquired after three weeks emulating
that man who nearly died at McDonalds,
his thirty days on fast food,
my three weeks on haute cuisine,
my own fault, of course,

unable to resist at each venue,
from a fancy hotel in Cape Town
to a posh safari camp in Kruger,
each eager to prove that Africa can still appeal
to the latest generation of Western wastrels,
those eager to relive the high life
of British bwanas in colonial guise,

those eager to take
more than their fair share,
as proffered by white entrepreneurs
on tables set by the dark hands
of Precious, Happiness, and Joy.

Would I rather
their parents had named them
Anger, Vengeance, and Bile?

Weighed down by recent experience
and ample knowledge of the past,
I give them my thanks
and take up my fork.

THE SECOND TIME

No one should listen to Brahms
the first time, it has been said,
or read a poem, or view Picasso
before a look at Masaccio, Michelangelo,
Titian, van Gogh or Monet.

Sophistication comes not all at once,
nor does a complex work of art
or a subtle idea sit on the table
like a piece of fruit. To be blind
or blinkered at first is no surprise,

and not so bad, if eyes later open.
Each reader, viewer or auditor
can heighten the pleasure of a second time,
if the second time might offer
a once-hidden something more,

like Brahms, Mark Twain,
a child's fairytale,
or a good second marriage.

TINTERN TO BRECON

Schooled by the master,
who taught the pantheon of nature,
I awoke to Tintern Abbey one morning,
Brecon Beacons the next, and though the former
touts a single God and reveals a human hand,
the stones, their tongues dulled
by centuries of quiet,
speak much of nature now,
an eloquent, sad voice, perhaps,
both godly man and the father God
quieter than once.

Then at Brecon this dawn,
no humans in sight,
only birds spoke to me,
birds plus lambs calling out
to separate and organize their mothers
on beautiful, replicating hills,
hills otherwise mute, except when I discover
runes speaking in some foreign tongue,
dark green, sinuous lines
drawn on a bright green earth,
shaping the landscape for my pleasure,
but for human purpose,

none of which I could find
in the stars last night,
stars in a plenitude suggesting
light years falling all upon themselves
to arrive all at once for our pleasure.

Revealing what? Wordsworth's pantheon,
perhaps, harmonious, benign,
though not quite as optimistic
as the flat screen down the pub last night,
small reptiles picking flies
off the rheumy eyes of lazy seals,

birds grooming the legs of rhinos,
nature gone all soft, no tooth, no claw,
but somehow just right
for Wordsworth, Tintern, and the Brecon Beacons.

SINGING THE BLUES IN BERLIN

Two ladies sang the blues,
looking very like Aretha,
two large ladies from Atlanta,
with voices to match,
proving their bona fides
by out-singing their band
and giving the mostly German crowd
what it came to hear,

especially a man I can't forget,
tall, bald, bullet-headed,
jowls and belly betraying the youthfulness
he must once have had, somewhere in the past.
He wept, with what memories
I can only guess—a trip to America,
jazz clubs in his youth, a lover,
a bordello in New Orleans?

He stood quietly in the rain,
having mounted a bench to overlook the umbrellas,
all rapt attention. Occasionally, with a quiver in his chin,
he wiped away tears, not just the rain,
as did I.

QUESTIONED AT SCHIPHOL

Dark eyes peered from under brown curls
as she inquired where we slept last night,
if we had packed our own bags,
whether any friend had asked us
to carry a package—this extra, individual
interrogation, by a special security agent,
almost like when we flew El Al,

except that this young woman did not look
as if she could bite through nails,
or as if she might want to,
almost immediately noting our
tanned faces, suggesting we must have had
a nice holiday, going on to remark

that she does not put her pretty face
under the sun much anymore,
since she gets home too tired from work,
but we all need the sun,
at least fifteen minutes a day,
as she learned from the doctor on Oprah,
with eighty-five percent of us in the West,
or maybe it was seventy-five percent,
having a deficiency in vitamin D,
even Oprah herself,

and vitamin D is good for the bones,
helping protect against that, oh yes, osteoporosis.
Calcium pills are good, but one should be careful
to see that magnesium is combined in the pills,
since calcium alone can make for trouble,
trouble in the rest room, you know,
as she learned, since it hardens,
but magnesium, she thinks it is magnesium,
loosens, and that takes care of it.

I enjoyed the ten minutes,
since we had arrived on time,

though not quite certain whether it represented
a carefully-trained regimen,
a clever way to loosen terrorist tongues,
or merely the way she gets through her day.

MONEY: FOUR DEGREES
OF SEPARATION

It was not so long ago
we went from seashells
to gold, then gold to paper,

so that I, for example,
have never carried gold,
but know the story, or myth,
of Fort Knox,

as my grandchildren might
learn to know the story, or myth,
of paper, before it was
replaced by plastic,

and now the plastic
can be replaced
by two smart phones
kissing one another,

with a computer program,
somewhere, juggling the numbers,
keeping track, so that my numbers
go up and yours go down,

or vice versa, the only question
being who gets to decide
when and how often
all of our numbers go up,

say by five per cent, the juggling
of numbers, sight unseen, by then
our worldwide method of exchange.
Will there still be a place

where bushels of paper dollars
are stacked like bales of hay
in a monumental barn?
Think of the cost of storage.

DERIVATIVES

"Bundles will not break," they said,
almost quoting Mussolini on twigs,
"this or that bad debt, collateralized,
cannot cause trouble,"

and they saw no trouble,
those who bundled the debt, for a fee,
those who sold the debt, minutes
before or after they bought it, for a fee,
those who sent their minions after future debtors,
good, bad, and indifferent, for a fee.
"Ask not what they earn,
or if they will pay,
but whether they will sign
on the dotted line."

And when we examine those dots,
what can we connect?
What did we derive
from the rise of Ronnie R,
from the Republican ascendancy,
from the heady belief that greed is good,
from Dubya's comfortable snuggle
in the rich man's pocket?

A collapse of the public good
for private gain,
a looting of the land
by the well connected,
a crash course in Coolidge,
with hopes for a new FDR
to fill the vacuum
and Hoover up the damage.
Derivatives.

ATLAS SHRUGGED

He read Ayn Rand,
for pity's sake,
a pitiless primer
for swashbuckling men
whose libertarian ideal
allows rapid ascent to the strong,
those who step on prone bodies,
Ayn Rand, for God's sake,
our lowbrow Nietzsche,

and this guru Greenspan,
the mastermind who never saw
a bubble he did not like,
finally noticed the irrational exuberance
had been his own, finally looked
at the rubble of his latest bubble,
finally saw the swash buckle,
and then our guru shrugged,
"Greed in the market
does not self-correct.
I was wrong."

NAMES AND ADDRESSES

Driving snow-covered roads,
Poland, mid-January, I see a sign
for Josefow, the small town
where "ordinary men" on July 13, 1942,
undertook the murder of fifteen hundred Jews,
one long day's work, and I am shocked to know
that Poles today must live there still,
must give Josefow as their home address,
shocked to realize that this name and this place
were not swallowed up and left only
to the pages of terrible books.

Then I find the few small homes
in the village of Treblinka,
the scattered houses in Sobibor,
having already seen the substantial town
of Terezin, once a deadly model ghetto,
now populated, presumably, by normal Czechs,
and, near the close of this trip, I reach
the houses, hotels, the shopping mall,
and the billboard for Kentucky Fried Chicken
in the booming city of Oswiecim,
known also as Auschwitz.

Road signs to Kielce might not
attract the attention of most,
unless they recognize it as the place
where sixty Jews were murdered,
not in 1944, but in 1946,
not by Germans, but by Poles, for the temerity
of finding their way home, after local residents,
several years before, had plundered their possessions.

Each name on a sign or in an address,
each community stained by the past,
seems jarring, almost too cruel to imagine,
but my shock is surely naive. Eighty million,

after all, give their address today
and live in that place still signposted
Deutschland. I even like going there.

That delicate balance between "never forget"
and "try not to remember" is far from easy.

ZAUBERBERG

I sit on my own Magic Mountain,
five floors above the flatlands of Moabit,
the flatlands of Berlin, where the highest hills
are those made of rubble, gathered after the bombing,
Teufelberg, for example, the Devil's Mountain,
a fitting name for rubble left behind by Adolf,
he who took the easy way out, without having to join
the "rubble women" picking up bricks, without having
to sweep the streets clean of bodies and blood,
that man many label demonic, a tool of Mephistopheles,
but I see as human, all too human, supported by
his human, all too human, scarred and petulant enablers,
in their enormous self-pity handing back
their sense of injustice to the rest of the world,
tenfold or more,

and just as Thomas Mann described it, before all that,
in his take on a Davos clinic against disease,
I sit on my early-morning balcony,
wrapped in warm clothing,
breathing the cool, fresh, health-giving air,
no B-17s or Lancaster bombers in sight or sound,
gazing out at the quiet mountain peaks of *Wohnhäuser*,
the golden Angel of Victory on the far horizon
celebrating the last actual victory at arms
experienced by my neighbors here, or their forebears,

and I ponder. I ponder life. I ponder my chance
to recover from this three months of self-induced musing,
some work, some play, some thoughts devoted
to the death sentence we call our three score and ten,
a number now drawing near,
but frequently surpassed today,
a death sentence mostly out of sight
for most of us, most of the time,

and I ponder the opportunity to read
more of Thomas Mann,
to put a few more words of my own to paper,
savoring the good things—this view from my balcony,
this mild autumn weather awash in blue—
hoping against hope that my fellow humans and I
might learn to beat back the disease
and leave a little less rubble in our wake,
though rubble is one of the things we do quite well.

EISBEIN MIT KRAUT

Eisbein mit Kraut,
a plate resonant
with Germans at their meat,
the joint, the dull red flesh,
the fat, the skin, the few dark hairs
of a once active swine,
knuckles saved
for another dish,

and I thank the gods
for my ascetic practice,
caprese salad, Pinot Grigio,
a clear palate.

Only when
my German counterpart
cuts away the fatty bits,
plus slabs of thick skin, placing all
on a side plate to be removed,

only then do I want to stake a claim,
add a side to my salad,
grab my portion of the pig
before a server comes
to take it all away.

NARCISSUS ON HOLIDAY

Self-consciously I stroll,
fully aware of the boots I wear,
neither cowboy boots—passé—
nor hiking boots—first cousin
to the Birkenstock—
but snub-nosed, lace-up boots,
nearly certain proof
of intellectual attachment
to the working classes,
nostalgic reminder
of a sweat-of-my-brow summer
half a lifetime ago.

Self-consciously I peruse
my pre-faded blue jeans,
just the right shade—not pre-torn
and over-priced; I scorn that sort of thing—
and I'm forced to admire
the subtle, slate-blue color
of my pullover shirt,
textured like long underwear,
hinting at après-ski in Aspen,
just right for fresh spring breezes
here on the Oregon coast.

Self-consciously self-satisfied,
I stroll, looking askance
at boomers too carefully dressed,
hair too carefully coiffed,
camouflage, I'm sure,
for lives too carelessly lived.

SO IRONIC WE MIGHT RUST

We're so ironic
we might rust in the rain.

Having given up on assertion,
fearful of seeming naive,
recognizing the unlikelihood
that any single claim
to truth or meaning
can withstand its rivals,
we ice our opinions
in irony,

for we are the ones
once so naive as to think
our nation unsullied,
before learning of Wounded Knee
and the Middle Passage,
before hearing of Jim Crow
and Bull Connor,

before Vietnam and Dylan
taught us the safety
of ironic distance.

Let him who is without irony
cast the first stone.
Unfortunately, he already has,
and now a little rust
is the least of our worries.

BLUE JEANS AND THE
ELECTRIC GUITAR

Some bright young scholar
centuries from now,
seeking the source
of American power,

will discover blue jeans
spread round the globe,
under dashikis, under white robes,
on men and women alike,
worn with the ubiquitous tee,
slogans and adverts in English,

will discover electric guitars
played by Tuareg bands in Niger,
electric guitars in Bali and Brazil,
electric guitars buried several layers above
terra cotta warriors in China,

and this bright young scholar will ask
the sensible question—how many divisions
did the Pentagon employ to bring about this victory,
how many missiles and smart bombs, at what cost?—

only to discover, to her surprise,
the many tasks botched by the Pentagon,
mishandled by its commander-in-chief,
Vietnam misunderstood, as it was laid waste,
Iraq torn asunder, as American power
raised up and nurtured its bitterest foes,

only to discover the soft power
behind blue jeans and electric guitars,
only to discover soft power
in the Declaration of Independence,
as quoted by Ho Chi Minh,
only to discover soft power

the American political elite,
the military-industrial complex,
and the baffled substrata of voters
could not.

YPRES

Sleeping quietly
opposite the Cloth Hall at Ypres,
now fully restored, some three hundred yards
from the salient, no shells bursting tonight,

having trod the grounds
at Talbot House in Poperinghe,
climbing the steep wooden steps
to Padre Clayton's chapel in the attic,
where he wheezed out old hymns
on a pump organ, offered wry wit,
distraction, and thoughts of home,
shook the hands of men,
some fated fraction about to die,

I nurture thoughts nudged
by the detritus of war
gathered here for my benefit,
bits of ragged brass now disinterred,
old maps, field glasses,
frightened words sent home to mum,
angry words shared with friends,
and with posterity, by trench poets
immortalized by their mortality,
their struggle toward honesty.

I thank the nearly one hundred years
that cushion me, leave me safe
in this place of death,
leave me wondering
how I and my fellows
can feel so threatened at the death
of three thousand, not ten million,
can call out the ugly dogs of war
and put the world at risk,
after all this.

LICKING OUR WOUNDS WITH A SEPTIC TONGUE

What if the cat has a septic tongue?
What if the cleansing lick of the tongue
only brings new germs to the wound?
What if the comforting, calming,
soothing, healing lick of the tongue
spreads a sore?
This is the making-it-worse verse:
what if we're making it worse?

Osama's tongue had a balming effect
for boys in the street, for Ataboy Atta
and other young boys whose wounds
were deep, wounds of race and pride,
a culture's wisdom so out of step
with hip hop, with rock and roll, with blue jeans,
so filled with righteous anger
against that which beckons, beckons,
just out of reach. But what if the tongue
has a septic effect? What if the young boys die?
What if their willingness coldly to kill
meets its match? What if seventy-two virgins
for each boy are not really waiting on the other side?
This is the making-it-worse verse:
what if he's making it worse?

George, George, you found your voice,
"smoke 'em out," "dead or alive," "bring 'em on,"
your tongue no longer licking only
the fundaments of the corporate world,
but soothing the wounds of the people,
hoping to calm and comfort
with the sweet honey of revenge
and the balm of righteous retribution.
When will we know the septic effect?
When will the joys of disproportionate war

turn back upon us, turn loose
the white-hot anger, make us
regret our pleasure in this ongoing war?
This is the making-it-worse verse:
what if we're making it worse?

THE KNUCKLEBALL

The knuckleball floats
so slowly toward the plate
that every knucklehead
thinks it the one pitch
he could hit,

not the cut fastball,
the sharp slider,
the split-finger, or
the hundred-mile-an-hour heat,

but that slowly approaching,
wholly enticing floater,
our knucklehead not quite believing
that it can break sharply
to left or to right,
not quite understanding
why even the best professionals
awkwardly swing and miss
more often than not.

After Germany, Russia,
and even Vietnam,
Iraq must have looked
like a knuckleball
to that Texas Ranger,
and to those chums of his dad,
those who had struck out,
walked, or reached by error,
and now clamored
for another at bat.

MELOS, MY LAI, ABU GHRAIB

The suit in steel-gray hair
was made to squirm,
peering through rimless glasses,
eyeing his accusers:
"What, do you think we are Nazis?"

Pictures from the Internet,
many strategically blurred
to protect the squeamish,
had to be denied,

these "disgusting acts,
perpetrated by criminals,
a few bad apples,
who will be found and punished,
for we don't tolerate
this sort of thing,"

meaning, presumably,
the taking of photos,
so cameras have now been banned,

but documents leak out
listing the forms of torture
approved by the steel-gray suit,
documents leak out
torturing the language of torture,
documents leak out
relegating quaint notions
of international law
and congressional decree
to the past, before it became necessary

to show those Melians
they could not defy Athens,
which invented democracy,
for God's sake,

to show those My Laians
they could not share
the dark skin and duplicitous tongue
of the Viet Cong and expect simply
to lie down, cower, cover their babies
and not be shot,

and if the Koran decrees
that Muslim men are shamed above all
by nakedness, public immodesty,
and if that, plus sleeplessness,
leering women, barking dogs
straining toward their genitals,
and specific, cramped or stretched
positions, enforced for hours,

if that might help
make these dogs talk,
and if poorly trained
night guards from West Virginia,
who might not have read the Koran,
can yet be made to administer
some nightly softening up,

no one should equate
the musings put down on paper,
the policy options discussed,
the purely literary imaginings
to be found in *Mein Kampf*
with the sordid and disgusting crimes
of those West Virginians.

COLOR COMMENTARY ON
AMERICAN WARS

When you speak of color
and American wars,
you've nearly said it all,
from sixteen oh seven in Virginia
and sixteen twenty in New England
to our war on black and brown children
in still-segregated schools, on urban streets,

with white-on-white wars
the easiest to justify, the easiest
to laud, to scan for heroes,
first against England, then Germany,
even the Civil War, if you side with the North
and can praise it for ending slavery,

but that massacre of Narragansets,
perpetrated by Pilgrims, that massacre
of Pequots, perpetrated by Puritans,
those Indian Wars of the nineteenth century,
with land grabs, that string of solemn promises
and signed treaties broken when shown to be
inconvenient, and with the cutting off of body parts
to keep for souvenirs. Our wars against red
require seriously averted eyes
if we're to sleep at night,

and our wars on yellow stretch
from the Chinese Exclusion Act
to Japanese Relocation, followed
by a criminal pursuit of Vietnamese
on false pretenses, "gooks" thrown
out of helicopters to make them talk,
massacred at My Lai, murdered
in free-fire zones, bombed, napalmed,

our wars on brown beginning
with that land-grab against Mexico
and moving to Iraq and Afghanistan,
"ragheads" easy to kill with our
asymmetrical tactics and skills,
easy to justify after nine eleven,
that minor incident on the scales
of modern wars, that yet rocked us so fully
off our belief in international law,
our sense of proportion,

and, finally, our wars on black,
beginning with the transport of Africans
in the holds of sailing ships,
continuing now with our record of
racist housing, racist school districts,
racist incarceration, racist capital punishment,
and the long list of black boys
stopped and questioned by the police,
unarmed black boys shot and killed by the police,
with a majority of white America
refusing to believe, apparently,
that any of this is based upon race,

a majority of white America
wanting to take the color
out of our commentary on war.

SIMPLE TRUTHS

I

Simple truths simply professed,
should that not be enough,
thought the teacher,
the man of words and books?

But he had not reckoned with
emotion, prejudice,
the love one bears
for the ideas of one's youth,

and, more than ideas,
for the comfort of privilege
and the familiar,

so that simple ideas
of truth and justice
will always struggle against
self-interest, advantage,
the holding on to what one has.

II

Simple truths simply confessed,
should that not be enough,
thought the preacher,
the man of words and books?

But he had not reckoned with
doubters and critics,
those who see in his simple truths
the bonds of dogma,

and, more than dogma,
the justification for privilege and hate,
the very license to kill,

so that every preacher
bears in his baggage
the blood of generations
and the curse of cant.

III

Simple truths simply expressed,
should that not be enough,
thought the aging intellectual,
the man of words and books?

But he had not reckoned with
those who insist the modern
is not today, but in the past,
those who question all,

those who argue
about what "is" is
and doubt that any truth
exists sans power,

so that our aging intellectual
has only the Kierkegaardian leap
and suffers much
of the graveyard angst
of old Churchyard himself.

NOTE TO SELF: HYDRATE

Those who would pee robustly
are well advised to hydrate,
take on liquids, amplify
the source for renal flow,

and yet I go
for days on end
without the quaff
of heightened word,

reading only the New York Times,
or some prattle about Bismarck,
googling Bleichröder, his Jewish friend,
or ogling that Bismarck of another sort
in the bakery window.

Whence the imaginative word,
I ask myself at four a.m.,
probing the meaning of life.
How to feed the flow?
Whom or what to know?

REMEMBERING WALT

In my lifelong cuddle with words,
I've been loath to label it poetry,
for the fuzzy lines which flowed from my pen
rarely took the form of a sonnet,
and then primarily in jest,

since I had quickly learned that verse
in quatrain or couplet,
or the music of Hiawatha,
though it could charm a child,
did not match in esteem or heft
the blanks fired by that shorter fellow, Walt,

the bewhiskered one, who could alarm and frighten
ladies and men who listened too closely,
so that Allen Ginsberg would later claim
to have slept with the man who slept with the man
who slept with the man who slept with the man,

and no one knows for certain
if that circle is real or broken,
but there lies within the words of Walt
the likelihood, or even the assurance,
that simple honesty broke out upon the page,

that lines splashed upon a page
had flowed straight from the heart,
down the poet's arm through an artery unknown to
science,
a free-flowing artery lacking the twists and turns,
the buffers and restraints which slow and stifle,

that Walt blurted out upon the page
truths never to be uttered over tea,
and so might we.

THE DICKINSON EFFECT

If one could choose
posthumous fame,
being rendered a giant in death,
or be thought moderately clever
while still alive,

would one prefer
the flush of ego in the moment
or the unexpected adjustment,
the pinch of salt,
the complex blending
of subtle herbs
vouchsafed to worms?

To taste it oneself
or to give pleasure at table?

I am not sure Emily Dickinson
can fully appreciate
that we feast upon her now,
or fully recognize
how good she tastes.

THE HEMINGWAY CODA

In every burst of short words,
first burst to last,
percussive by preference,
mostly one or two slabs,
there can be music,
meaning to follow,
if we're lucky,
but even the worst burst,
short, hard-edged,
okay if we're not.

Martial? Often.
Atavistic? Quite.
Embarrassing? Maybe,
but no more
than any four-dollar word
where one dollar would do.

DID THEY DO IT TOO?

"And there I shut her wild wild eyes with kisses four."
John Keats, 1820

With kisses four, not less, not more?
Perhaps it was to rhyme with sore
Keats chose these words
and nothing more

as he described his Knight at arms,
and I should read without alarms
enkindled in my modern mind,
it only harms,

for maybe when La Belle Dame
looked at him and made sweet moan,
it was merely a platonic scene
I could describe to Mom.

The honey wild and manna dew
and her strange tongue should not construe
that they two centuries ago
would do what some today might do,

but when the Knight used kisses four
to close two eyes, though wild and sore,
my mind immediately sought out
two places more.

A RIFF ON PAUL

Yea, though I speak
in the tongues of birds, even angels,
will I find love as other poets do?

When I seek out heavenly words
and find only clanging symbols,
will others like me?

Love is not boastful.
It should not circumnavigate
pretentious circumlocutions,

but my locutions
of every kind
seem difficult to navigate.

"Locute, locute, it will be so cute,"
said my teacher in this biz,
alas, a clanging cymbal,

so that only when
I turned to prose
did the pros take notice,

and the bird that mattered
sang back to me.

REAL POETRY

Thoughts pressed like a Porsche
into a paperweight,

distilled like vodka,
spuds with the kick of a horse,

desiccated, freeze-dried,
words few in number:
add water and stand back.

SMITTEN

Smitty, Smitty,
sometimes smutty,
wordsmith of my youth,

often pithy,
rarely puffy,
my arbiter of couth.

Camouflage,
half mirage,
his words could be a veil,

decoration,
peroration,
scalpel or a nail.

PROPER POESY?

Should a poem
be tight as a fist,
smooth as a nectarine,
filled near to bursting
with sweet fruit?

Or could we call it a poem
when it more resembles
dirty laundry, a random,
unremarkable, slightly
aromatic collection
of socks and underwear?

The choice is ours.

LES MURRAY, MORE MATTER

[On reading a *New Yorker* review, "Fire Down Below,"
        by Dan Chiasson, June 11 and 18, 2007]

There's an Aussie bloke
whose hard life with words,
whose hard life and hard words
make me feel, for a moment,
that which he seems not to feel,

though a poet, one of the best,
meant to be a genius at feeling,
one might think, instead

astringent, nearly autistic,
hurt by poverty, hurt by young girls
who made him yearn
then staunched his yearning,

until a chicken bone
pierced his gut, spread poison,
gave him twenty days in Christ's tomb
before his resurrection.

A nicer fellow now,
with traces of empathy,
one word in ten
cooling the scorching sun
on the tin roof of his brain
with the bare whisper
of an evening breeze.

LOUIS AND THE *ARS POETICA*

When we ponder the poetic arts
here in Kitsap County,
we think of Louis, he who
nudged, nourished, and noodled
a little poetry into generations
of students, each face remembered,
each name, each subsequent career,
each present location,

our Louis, this man with a famously tin ear,
banished from college French
for congenital mispronunciation,
Louis, who cannot sing a note,
who claims not to know a bass from a tenor,
a hawk from a handsaw,

and yet a man with plenty of time
for William and the dolorous Dane,
time for rolling well-shaped words
over his tongue, savoring their succulence,
tasting Milton, tasting Donne,
tasting Emily Dickinson,

now full of years, ensconced
in leisure's garden of delights,
sipping the water of life,
stroking Stormy the Cat,
sitting in a comfortable chair
and resting on his *ars poetica*.

GRAVITY

My friend Phil
says gravity's
the great enemy,
tugging at our dignity,
tugging at those
portions of our flesh
which once held firm,

filling the pouches
under our eyes,
doubling our chins,
wreaking havoc
on our torsos,
until some of us
come to resemble
our own teardrops.

Such an enemy,
subtle, relentless,
and though we might begin
like a young Alexander,
victories diminish over time,

some giving up early,
some fighting on,
but the outcome
never in doubt:

unable to stand
for battle,
we will lie prone,
and gravity
will turn on our heirs.

GOOD FRIDAYS

And yet we call it good,
ironically, this day of death,
thank God it's here again,
this signal of the end.

We celebrate the seven days,
the seven words, fear that
we too need forgiveness,
know not what we do, except we thirst,

and we tire, as did God,
he who invented the day of rest
after each week's work,
our Sabbath, our sabbatical.

Each Friday good, most welcome,
for we crave rest, relief,
we who are ever more in need
of an afternoon nap

as the years pass over,
as we tire, feel the need to re-tire,
or at least re-cap, add some rubber,
some resilience for the road ahead.

SLIPSTREAMING

Caught in the slipstream,
pushed by the tradewinds,
all sails engaged,
no chance, it seems,
to ascend the rigging
and drop a sheet,

wishing at times
for a few days becalmed,
another birthday approaching,
thoughts of port,
aware of finitude.

RETRAIN OR RETIRE?

I retire every night,
collapsed in exhaustion,
and I awake each morning,
ears ringing like the green chain end
of a timber mill,

and so I think it's time
to ponder the wisdom of Eric Idle,
a man whose very name
is an inspiration,
he who wrote
on the meaning of life.

It is time to wonder
whether to weather the weather
of another Puget Sound winter,
or perhaps greet the spring
in the bosom of Palm Springs.

It is time to think
one could retire, actually,
take that sabbatical without end,
or, rather, that sabbatical
with only one end,
the box that awaits even those
most eager to think outside the box.

Perhaps I should retrain,
given the longevity of boomers,
but that seems a strain.
I think I'll retire.

NINTH INNING IN PANKOW

A Friday night at Bier in Pankow,
BIP, as it calls itself,
sitting next to a party of several old men,
men remembering the GDR,
reminders of which I also have noted
in this corner of old Berlin,
the un-renovated buildings,
the broken plaster
on my building's façade,
the lack of a Commerzbank at hand,
until I take a tram toward the West.

Alles hat geklappt in terms
of my arrival, finding my way
to the flat, meeting Frau Wunnicke,
being pleasantly surprised
by the size of the rooms,
their light and airy charm.

Now I drink a beer and ponder life,
my good fortune, the pleasant surprise
of recent, unexpected accolades,
the several invitations, all of this
in what must be considered
the bottom of the ninth inning.

Having caught up from behind,
I now can imagine extra innings,
perhaps even a walk-off home run,
a walk-off of some sort in any case.

THE GRATEFUL DEAD

Jerry Garcia, now, once again,
one of the grateful dead,
or so we might hope,
as I also hope for my father,

pondering with pleasure
their recent first meeting,
Dad no doubt attracted first
by the tie, reminding him, perhaps,
of that chartreuse number
now resting its kinetic charge
in the dark closet
of my younger brother John,

the brother who helped teach Dad,
some time ago, to accept with equanimity
grooming choices like those affected
by his new friend Jerry,
and also by God himself,
if some of the portraits
have gotten it right.

DANSE MACABRE

Seeking out a place to die,
heading south to the desert,
knowing we might retire
in a few years, if the
Boomer Depression were to allow,

we dance our way
into the sere desert of Palm Springs,
sere, though hardly austere,
given the ghost of Liberace,
the ratatat echo of the Rat Pack,
the robust memory of Kate Smith,
her one hundred golden goblets,
signed portraits, and other memorabilia
mirroring the taste of another day,
all on sale this weekend, along with
her Spanish hacienda at two mill.

We bought a gold leaf portrait
of young Kate, not yet filling out her frame,
a portrait proving she was young once,
as were we, she who came to the desert to die,
despite a bronze sculpture beside the pool,
dedicated to her indomitable spirit,
despite the two candelabra lighting her way,
supported by porcelain servants in black face,
despite the large record collection and her prayer
that God might bless America,

and we will now decide
if Palm Springs might be the place
where we too shall try
eventually to die.

OBIT IN THE TIMES

He worked in The City,
she worked the West End.
He once played for England,
she played all the best men.
He cheated death
for another six months.
She cheated his heirs,
or so they said in court,
though no one could report
a frown on his face
in those last days.

He who'd taken a wicket for England
in India, another in Cape Town,
had now taken a wicket for himself,
three legs left standing,
jubilation all 'round,
a small redistribution of wealth,
she a landowner in France,
he with a small English plot
entirely sufficient to his needs.

TABLE OF CONTENTS

When I sidle up
to my table of contents,
I see ten fingers and ten toes,
two arms, two legs,
and I could see
the contents of my stomach
had it been pumped,

yet each of us wants more,
I think, and there nuance
is in wax, empirical certainty
on the wane,

so that the contents on my table,
when arrayed for viewing—
a few words in print,
some old bills,
dog-eared statements
from the bank—
will likely produce assessments
mirroring their present variety,

unless, when the time comes,
tears soften sight
like Vaseline on a lens.

About the Author

RP Ericksen holds a PhD in History and is the author of the political commentary, *The Left Has Always Been Right*, as well as a number of publications on German history. Born and raised in the Pacific Northwest, he savors a close network of family and friends, most of whom tolerate his pondering.

Printed in the United States
By Bookmasters